DISCOVER
ANCIENT
MESOPOTAMIA

DISCOVER ANCIENT CIVILIZATIONS

DISCOVER ANCIENT MESOPOTAMIA

Stephen Feinstein

Enslow Publishers, Inc.
40 Industrial Road
Box 398
Berkeley Heights, NJ 07922
USA

http://www.enslow.com

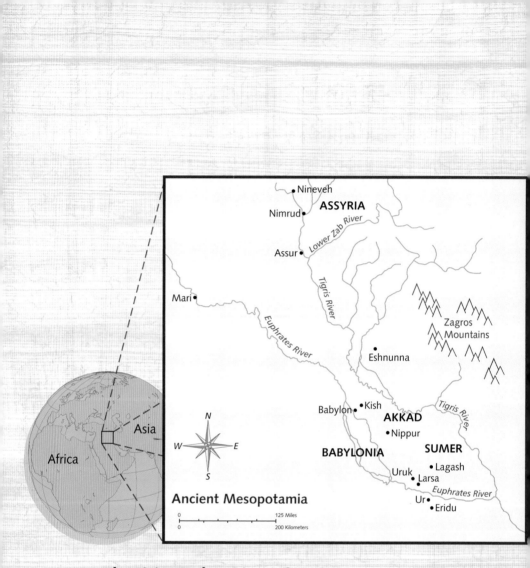

The cities and empires of ancient Mesopotamia are shown on this map.

Ruins of the ancient city of Nippur, which were once excavated, are becoming hidden again by desert storms.

Title was originally published as *Ancient Mesopotamia* in 2005.

No part of this book may be reproduced by any means
without the written permission of the publisher.

Library of Congress Cataloging-in-Publication Data

Feinstein, Stephen.
    Discover ancient Mesopotamia / Stephen Feinstein.
       p. cm. — Discover ancient civilizations)
    Includes bibliographical references and index.
    Summary: "Learn about the art and cultural contributions, family life, religions and people
       of ancient Mesopotamia"—Provided by publisher.
    ISBN 978-0-7660-4197-4
    1. Iraq—History—To 634—Juvenile literature. I. Title.
    DS71.F455 2014
    935—dc23

                          2012011573

Future editions:
Paperback ISBN 978-1-4644-0337-8   Single-user PDF ISBN 978-1-4646-1188-9
ePUB ISBN 978-1-4645-1188-2   Multi-user PDF ISBN 978-0-7660-5817-0

Printed in the United States of America

112013 Lake Book Manufacturing, Inc., Melrose Park, IL

10 9 8 7 6 5 4 3 2 1

To Our Readers: We have done our best to make sure all Internet Addresses in this book were active and appropriate when we went to press. However, the author and the publisher have no control over and assume no liability for the material available on those Internet sites or on other Web sites they may link to. Any comments or suggestions can be sent by e-mail to comments@enslow.com or to the address on the back cover.

♻ Enslow Publishers, Inc., is committed to printing our books on recycled paper. The paper in every book contains 10% to 30% post-consumer waste (PCW). The cover board on the outside of each book contains 100% PCW. Our goal is to do our part to help young people and the environment too!

Photo Credits: © Enslow Publishers, Inc., pp. 5; © 2012 Photos.com, a division of Getty Images. All rights reserved., pp. 11, 20, 27, 42-43, 45, 53; U. S. Army photo by Staff Sgt. Garrett Ralston, p. 13; Joel Carillet/© 2012 Photos.com, a division of Getty Images. All rights reserved., pp. 16-17; Clipart. com/© 2012 Photos.com, a division of Getty Images. All rights reserved., pp. 26, 59, 60, 87; Huseyin Clionem Celikkol /© 2012 Photos.com, a division of Getty Images. All rights reserved., pp. 30-31; Photo courtesy of the U.S. Air Force: Photographer Staff Sgt. Scott Gaitley, 931st Air Refueling Group historian, pp. 32-33; Shutterstock, pp. 36, 46, 62-63, 88-89; Dorling Kindersley RF/Thinkstock, pp. 57, 83, 91; Fabio Bianchini/© 2012 Photos.com, a division of Getty Images. All rights reserved., p. 65; Anthony Baggett/© 2012 Photos.com, a division of Getty Images. All rights reserved., pp. 70-71, 76; © Dover Publications, p. 73; U.S. Air Force photo by Staff Sgt. JoAnn S. Makinano, pp. 78, 80-81; Michael Spencer/Saudi Aramco World/PADIA, pp. 6, 25, 51.

Front Cover: Sculpture: © 2012 Photos.com, a division of Getty Images. All rights reserved.;
Enameled tile of lion: Shutterstock

Table of CONTENTS

Caucasus Mts

Indo Europeans

CASPIAN
SEA

ain Land of
A or HALDIA

ds of
A

Chapter 1

MESOPOTAMIA:
LAND BETWEEN
the RIVERS

Tris River

rain of Shinar

Sumer

Nippur

Lagash

Larsa

.Susa

Ur

Chaldean
Marsh-lands

Highlands
of ELAM

Highlands
of PERSIA

SEA OF THE RISING SUN

PERSIAN GULF

The land that we now call Iraq was known as Mesopotamia thousands of years ago. The ancient Greeks gave it that name, which means "between the rivers,"— *meso*, "between," and *potamos*, "river."[1] Mesopotamia did indeed lie between two rivers—the Tigris and the Euphrates. The two rivers begin in the eastern mountains of what is now Turkey. The Tigris flows southeastward into Iraq while the Euphrates flows south into Syria before veering toward the southeast and crossing into Iraq. After the Tigris has traveled 1,180 miles and the Euphrates has traveled 1,700 miles, both rivers join together in southern Iraq at Al Qurnah. The combined river, known as the Shatt al Arab, flows 120 miles southeast to the Persian Gulf.

Mesopotamia is part of a larger area that is known to archaeologists and historians as the Fertile Crescent. This is a crescent-shaped area of land that extends

A modern view of the lands that were once ancient Mesopotamia. The space shuttle *Atlantis* flies above the Fertile Crescent. The Fertile Crescent can be seen in an upside-down "u" shape.

along the valley of the Tigris and Euphrates, west to the shores of the Mediterranean Sea, and then south to land of Egypt. The Fertile Crescent was home to several important early cultures and civilizations besides the Mesopotamians. The ancient Egyptians were one such civilization.

At first glance, the land of Mesopotamia might seem an unlikely setting for the development of the world's first civilizations. Much of Mesopotamia is a bleak, barren plain with a climate that makes life difficult. Most of the south and west is a desert wasteland that gets only about four to six inches of rainfall per year. The treeless grasslands in the north get about twelve to sixteen inches of rain annually, mainly in the spring. Higher amounts of rain fall in the mountains along the Iran-Iraq border and along the northern border. While winter temperatures can be surprisingly cold, summers are extremely hot, with temperatures often

Iraqi boys watch as water flows freely from the Tigris River into an irrigation canal in present-day Iraq, on November 14, 2010. The water was delivered through a pump station and feeds 1500 area farms.

rising above 120°F. Choking dust storms frequently sweep across the land. How, then, did such a place become the "cradle of civilization," as it has often been called?

The Development of Agriculture

Archaeologists have found the remains of Neanderthals, early humans, who lived in Mesopotamia during the last ice age. They discovered the forty-five-thousand-year-old skeletons in a cave at Shanidar in northern Iraq. The Neanderthals became extinct during the ice age, perhaps wiped out by people resembling modern humans. When the ice age ended, about twelve thousand years ago, small bands of nomadic hunter-gatherers, people who moved from place to place, wandered across northern Meso-potamia. They crossed the hills between the Zagros Mountains along the border of present-day Iraq and Iran and the northern Mesopotamian plains. The people lived in campsites and caves. The hunter-gatherers followed herds of wild animals, such as gazelles, deer, and aurochs, large wild oxen with horns. They also hunted goats and wild sheep in the mountains and wild boars in the marshes, and they ate the many edible plants of the region.

At some point, people in northern Mesopotamia learned how to grow crops and tame animals. Early farmers grew wheat, barley, peas, lentils, carrots, turnips, and leeks. They domesticated goats, sheep, pigs (from wild boar), and cattle (from aurochs). The development of agriculture brought about a change from a nomadic way of life to a settled lifestyle.

In the 1940s, Robert J. Braidwood, an American archaeologist, began excavating the remains of a nine-thousand-year-old village known as Jarmo in the hills of northern Mesopotamia. He found fifteen levels of habitation spanning about four

The Euphrates River and farmland as seen from Dura-Europos, Syria, a few miles north from where the river flows into Iraq.

hundred years. The upper layers included the remains of mud huts, stone tools, seeds, and broken pots. In the lower layers were crude stone hoes and cultivated grains. But agricultural methods, especially methods of irrigation, that were developed at Jarmo spread to other peoples living in the Tigris-Euphrates plain. It was this development that led to the rise of civilization in Mesopotamia.[2]

Settlement of Southern Mesopotamia

The first settlements in ancient Mesopotamia were mainly in the northern grasslands. There was enough rainfall for agriculture to develop and good grazing land to raise farm animals. Early cultures in the area included the Hassuna, Samarra, and Halaf. Each is characterized by its own type of pottery.

Beginning about 6500 B.C., groups of people from the north began migrating to southern Mesopotamia. Why were they attracted to a land with little rainfall and extremely hot weather? There was only one reason—the remarkably fertile land along the Tigris and Euphrates rivers. Each year in the spring, melting snows in the Zagros Mountains and other ranges flowed into the two rivers, causing them to overflow their banks. The yearly flooding, which had been going on for thousands of years, created natural levees, or raised embankments, of silt and sediment.[3] The levees, which drained easily, proved to be ideal for the planting and cultivation of crops such as wheat and barley. In addition, the reed-covered marshes nearby were filled with fish and waterfowl (such as ducks and geese) throughout much of the year.

It is not surprising, then, that before long, villages sprung up across the flood-plain of the Tigris-Euphrates (low-lying flood-prone area) in the southern part of

Mesopotamian Clay Tablet

Mesopotamia. From around 6500 B.C. to 4000 B.C., a culture known as the Ubaid flourished in the region. Ubaid farmers built mud-brick houses and temples and dug irrigation canals to bring water to their crops. As the villages grew, larger and more numerous farms and fields under cultivation required more extensive canals and reservoirs. Irrigation projects like these required the efforts of an entire community of people.

Villages that prospered through agriculture eventually grew into cities. The first major cities in southern Mesopotamia included Uruk, Eridu, Ur, Lagash, Nippur, and Kish. Uruk had an estimated population of about fifty thousand. During the Uruk period, people developed a way to keep track of their crops and animals. Archaeologists who excavated the site of ancient Uruk found more than five thousand clay tablets. Pictographs, pictures of animals, wheat, and other objects, were drawn on the tablets. Signs representing numbers were placed next to the pictures. While these pictographs were not yet a written language, they did signal a step in the development of writing. The achievements of the Uruk period paved the way for the development of the world's first civilization.

Indo Europeans

Caucasus Mts

CASPIAN
SEA

tain Land of
A or HALDIA

Tigris River

Plain of Shinar

Nippur

Lagash

Larsa

Sumer

Ur

Chaldean
Marsh-lands

Susa

Highlands
of ELAM

Highland
of PERSI

SEA OF THE RISING SUN

PERSIAN GULF

Chapter 2

SUMER:
The WORLD'S
FIRST
CIVILIZATION

Historians do not know exactly when the people known as Sumerians came to Mesopotamia—or even if they did, since they may have lived there from the beginning. But historians do know that by about 3000 B.C., the world's first civilization, known as Sumerian, had arisen in Mesopotamia, a land that then became known as Sumer. Ancient cities in the land, including Uruk, Eridu, Ur, Lagash, Nippur, and Kish, became the centers of powerful Sumerian city-states.

The World's First Written Language

In a sense, history began in Sumer with the beginning of writing, probably around 3000 B.C. The first writing was created by drawing pictures of animals, wheat, and other objects on soft, wet clay tablets. These pictures later developed into a more efficient system of writing. Using a stylus made from a cut reed with a wedge-shaped tip, Sumerian scribes made wedge-shaped marks in the clay. The clay tablet was then left to dry in the sun until it hardened. Clay tablets were flat and usually rectangular or square, but some were rounded.

The Sumerian writing system, the world's first, is known as cuneiform. The word *cuneiform* comes from a Latin word meaning "wedge-shaped."[1] Tens of thousands of clay tablets have been found by archaeologists. Every aspect of Sumer's economic life was recorded by scribes, or professional writers, on clay tablets. There were also the records of historical events, customs, and traditions. The earliest literary texts on clay tablets date from about 2400 B.C. Myths and epics, such as stories about the famous Sumerian king Gilgamesh, were written in cuneiform script. Poems, proverbs, and riddles were also recorded on clay tablets.

Clay envelope with clay tablet.

Around 2300 B.C., envelopes were invented. The envelopes were slips of clay formed around clay tablets. With the invention of envelopes, it became possible to send private letters. Sumerians used small disks and cylinders made of stone as personal seals. The impressions of the seals in clay served as signatures.

**Depiction of
Gilgamesh with lion**

Most people in Sumer could neither read nor write, so an organized system of education was necessary to train scribes. Schools were called tablet-houses, and students most likely came from the wealthiest families. Students had to learn to read and write about six hundred cuneiform signs. The learning process involved memorization, dictation, writing new lessons and reviewing old ones, reading aloud from written documents, and spelling. Students also had to study mathematics, science, literature, and grammar.

**Cuneiform Tablet Describing
Gilgamesh Flood Epic**

A Flourishing of the Arts

Students who graduated from the tablet-house became scribes, and these were almost always men. It was very rare for women to be scribes, but in Sumer, a woman who was a scribe was also likely to be a priestess. Enheduanna, a high priestess of the city-state of Ur, is the first recorded writer in history. She lived from about 2280 B.C. to 2220 B.C. and wrote a series of forty-two short hymns on clay tablets.[2] Her best-known poem, called the "Exaltation of Inanna," was written in honor of the Sumerian moon goddess. An ancient clay tablet inscribed in cuneiform referring to her parentage has led historians to believe that Enheduanna was the daughter of Sargon of Akkad, the powerful ruler of an empire in Mesopotamia.

Writing was undoubtedly the Sumerians' greatest achievement, but there were other important Sumerian inventions as well. These include the wheel (wagon wheel and potter's wheel), the sail, the plow, and a number system based on sixty—which is still used when measuring time and angles. Sumerian metalworkers discovered that they could melt copper and tin together to make sturdy objects. By about 2500 B.C., the Sumerians were producing copper alloy spearheads and body armor. Sumerian innovations in architecture included arches, columns, ramps, and the ziggurat.

Sumerian City-States

The original Ubaid towns where the Sumerians lived grew into larger urban centers built around temples. Within the temple complex in the center of each city was a ziggurat, a tall, stepped mud-brick tower. The word *ziggurat,* which comes from the Akkadian word *zigguratu,* means "peak, or high place."[3] A ziggurat consisted of several platforms built one on top of the other. Ramps and stairways led to each

Beehive homes can be found in the thick of hot deserts and desert cities. Most are found in rural farming communities, but there are even villages located in Aleppo, the largest city in Syria, which has been continually inhabited since the 6th millennium B.C. The Aleppo beehive homes are used both for storage and homes. The site of Harran, Syria has been occupied since at least the Ubaid period.

platform. At the top of the tower stood a temple dedicated to the god that was considered to be the protector of that city, since each Sumerian city had its own god. For example, Ur had Nanna, the moon god, while Eridu had Enki, the god of wisdom and sweet waters.

Sumerians believed that the welfare of their city depended on the favor of the gods, and the most important god was the particular god of each city. So during the first few hundred years of the Sumerian civilization, most aspects of life in the Sumer's cities, including economic, political, and cultural matters, were controlled by the temple.[4] The temple

Sumer: The World's First Civilization

between 2 and 3

The ziggurat of Nanna at Ur stands in the distance, while tombs of the royal family are in the foreground. Nanna was the moon god of the six-thousand-year-old royal city of Ur.

administrators oversaw the activities of Sumerian citizens from all walks of life: scribes, teachers, soldiers, merchants, government officials, potters, metalworkers, farmers, and weavers. Because the wool cloth was such an important part of the Sumerian economy, temple administrators even monitored the process by which raw wool was converted into cloth.

The major cities, where tens of thousands of inhabitants lived, extended their control over the surrounding region, becoming city-states. Each city-state included several smaller towns situated within the territory of the city-state. The city-state included fertile farmlands where farmers raised wheat, millet, barley, and vegetables such as peas, onions, lettuce, and turnips. They also included grazing lands, where shepherds tended herds of sheep, goats, and cattle.

Conflicts Lead to Kingship

By about 2800 B.C., conflicts broke out between city-states over disputes about land. As the warfare increased, rule by assemblies of citizens gave way to kingship, in which there was one king or ruler for each city-state. Eventually, kingship became hereditary, and dynasties, or families of rulers, were established. By 2500 B.C., one Sumerian king became so powerful that when he died, all of his royal attendants were buried along with him so that they could continue to serve him in the afterlife.

As each city-state became more vulnerable to a rival's attack, the city's walls were strengthened. Fortified walls were built with mud bricks, which were often baked on the outside of the wall and sun-dried on the inside. Stone was also used wherever possible. Gilgamesh, king of the Sumerian city of Uruk, proudly describes the strong walls he built around his city in this excerpt from *The Epic of Gilgamesh:*

> Climb up and walk the length of Uruk's walls. Inspect its foundation. Make trial of the brick. Were not the bricks hardened in fire? Did not the Seven Sages lay their course?[5]

Warfare between rival Sumerian city-states continued for about five hundred years. By 2350 B.C., the constant fighting

Head Statue of Ebih-il, Superintendent of Mari, ancient Iraq (circa 2400 B.C.). The statue's eyes have pupils inlaid with lapis lazuli. Small statues of Sumerians praying were probably place in temples dedicated to the city's god.

weakened the Sumerian civilization and made it vulnerable to conquest. The more powerful Akkadian civilization in the lands north of Sumer would take advantage of that weakness.

Chapter 3

AKKAD:
The WORLD'S FIRST EMPIRE

While the Sumerian civilization was developing and flourishing in southern Mesopotamia, a civilization known as the Akkadian followed a similar pattern in northern Mesopotamia. Like the people of Sumer, the Akkadians lived in villages and towns, raised crops, and in many ways shared the lifestyle, religious beliefs, and culture of the Sumerians. It is not known for certain whether the Akkadians organized their political or social life as the Sumerians did in their city-states. But there is no doubt that the Akkadians were influenced in many ways by Sumerian civilization. The major difference between the two groups was their language.

A Tale of Two Languages

The Akkadian and the Sumerian languages were completely unrelated—as different from each other as Latin and Chinese are. Akkadian was a Semitic language, and the

Hebrew and Arabic languages are related to the Akkadian language. The Sumerian language, on the other hand, is not like any other language in the world that we know of. Cuneiform writing was developed for Sumerian, but Akkadian scribes modified it so they could write their own language. This was a remarkable achievement, considering the vast differences in the two languages.

Over time, the Akkadians incorporated Sumerian words into their own language. The Sumerians, for their part, borrowed a smaller number of Akkadian words. Yet it was the Akkadian language that became the language spoken throughout Mesopotamia, and that happened because the Akkadians gained political power in the region. The Sumerian language would eventually become a "dead" one, used in literature and science but not commonly spoken. In later Mesopotamian civilizations, the Babylonians in southern Mesopotamia would speak one dialect of Akkadian, and the Assyrians in northern Mesopotamia would speak another dialect of Akkadian. Eventually, Akkadian was replaced by Aramaic, a Semitic language that became common in southwest Asia.[1]

Sargon the Great, King of Akkad

Sargon I, who would become king of Akkad, was born around 2350 B.C. According to legend, Sargon's mother had given birth to him in secret, and then placed him in a basket made of reeds and cast him adrift on the Euphrates River. The basket floated down the river until it was retrieved downstream by a farmer named Akki, who was drawing water from the river to irrigate his field. The farmer raised the Akkadian boy as his own son. This legend echoes the story in the bible about the origins of Moses. Some scholars think that the story in the

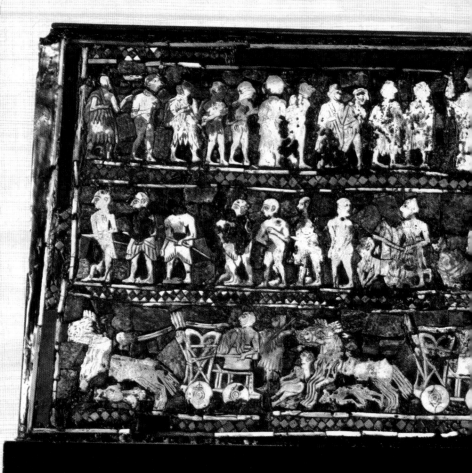

The Standard of Ur is a Sumerian artifact excavated from what had been the Royal Cemetery in the ancient city of Ur. It is approximately 4,500 years old and was probably constructed in the form of a hollow wooden box with scenes of war and peace represented on each side through elaborately inlaid mosaics. The main panels are known as "War" and "Peace."

The "War" panel shows one of the earliest representations of a Sumerian army. Chariots, each pulled by four donkeys, trample enemies; infantry with cloaks carry spears; enemy soldiers are killed with axes, others are paraded and presented to the king who holds a spear.

bible may very well have been based on the legend of Sargon.

As a young man, Sargon rose to a high position inside the royal court in the Sumerian city of Kish. He became cup-bearer to Ur-Zababa, the Sumerian king. This was a position of great honor in the ancient world, because only those who could be trusted would be given the responsibility of serving the king wine at his table.

The Akkadian Conquest of Sumer

But during a revolt in the palace, Sargon overthrew the king and seized the royal throne. After declaring himself king of Kish, Sargon set out to conquer the other city-states of Sumer. His armies were able to accomplish this through the use of a new weapon: the composite bow, used to launch arrows. The composite bow was made of wood, bone, and sinew glued together in

Sargon, king of Akkad, is generally given credit for building the world's first empire.

2 **Ancient Akkadian Life-size Copper Alloy Head of a Ruler, Cooper alloy; Early Bronze Age, c. 2300**

several layers instead of the single piece of wood used in the simple bow. This construction increased the strength of the bow and the speed and distance of the arrows it fired. By using a composite bow, archers could strike their targets while remaining out of reach of incoming arrows.[2] More advanced weapons give an army tremendous advantages on the battlefield. The use of the composite bow may have helped Sargon's forces gain quick victories over their Sumerian enemies.

By about 2334 B.C., Sargon had conquered Sumer and then brought all of Mesopotamia under his rule. He proved to be as good an organizer and administrator as he was a military leader. He appointed Akkadian governors in all the important Sumerian city-states. He destroyed the defensive walls of defeated Sumerian cities. The Akkadian language replaced Sumerian as the language of administrative records.

Sargon made the city of Agade his capital, building his royal palace there. Sargon wisely chose to respect Sumer's religious institutions, building temples in Agade and appointing his daughter Enheduanna the high priestess of Ur.

The World's First Empire

Sargon established the most extensive kingdom that Mesopotamia had ever seen. But he had only just begun on his path of conquest. Sargon wasted little time in launching major military campaigns. He sent his armies marching eastward toward present-day Iran and westward toward present-day Syria and Turkey. Beyond Mesopotamia's eastern borders, Sargon conquered a people known as the Elamites. In the west, his armies reached the Taurus Mountains near the Mediterranean coasts of Syria and Turkey. Sargon's chariots, foot soldiers, archers, and spearmen may even have ventured farther east, although some historians disagree on how far.

Sargon's armies met with quick success in many places. He was soon in control of a huge territory that extended through Syria and what is today Turkey as well as lands reaching the Mediterranean to the west and the Black Sea to the north. The lands ruled by Sargon are considered by many scholars to be the world's first empire.

Sargon controlled the supply routes in his lands, which he used to transport looted goods from conquered cities back to Agade, his capital. Sargon's sons formed a dynasty that ruled the empire after his death. Sargon believed that a powerful central authority controlling a large territory that included many different groups was the best system of government. This would become the model for many later Mesopotamian kingdoms and empires. Sargon's empire, however, lasted less than

Kish, a once-important Sumerian
city, now stands in ruins.

two hundred years. When Sargon died in 2279 B.C., his heirs were unable to hold the empire together.

The End of Sargon's Empire

Around 2200 B.C., the Akkadian Empire came to an end as some Sumerian city-states rebelled against their Akkadian rulers. The final blow came when a people known as the Gutians swept into Meso-potamia from the Zagros Mountains in present-day Iran and became the rulers of Mesopotamia.

The Gutians ruled Mesopotamia for at least the next fifty years. But by 2140 B.C., the Sumerians had begun to take back control of their cities. Gudea, the Sumerian king of the city of Lagash, began rebuilding the city's temples. In 2120 B.C., Utuhegal, the king of Uruk, drove the Gutians out of Sumer.[3] In 2112 B.C., Ur-Nammu became king of Ur and established what is now

Statue of Gudea, Prince of Lagash (c. 2150 B.C.) diorite. Gudea quickly rose to power after marrying Ninalla, daughter of the former ruler of Lagash. Gudea's influence was vast; temples built by Gudea in Ur, Nippur, Adab, Uruk, and Bad-Tibira all bear the prince's inscription.

called the Third Dynasty of Ur, which lasted for about one hundred years. This was the last important Sumerian dynasty.

During a period of unrest that followed, a Semitic people known as the Amorites, from what is today Syria, began moving into Mesopotamia. By around 2000 B.C., many Sumerian cities had fallen under their control. In the year 2000 B.C., a group of Elamites attacked and destroyed the city of Ur. Although the Amorites drove the Elamites out of Mesopotamia, Sumer ceased to exist as a political and economic force. But a new empire was about to be born among the old Sumerian cities.

Chapter 4

The BABYLONIAN EMPIRE

For more than two hundred years, Mesopotamia remained in constant upheaval. City-states under the control of Amorite kings were often in conflict with each other, just as in earlier times these same city-states under Sumerian rule had waged war against one another. Babylon, a small town on the banks of the Euphrates River, was captured in 1894 B.C. by an Amorite called Sumu-abum. He established a small kingdom with the city of Babylon as his capital. Babylon was located about fifty-six miles south of present-day Baghdad.

Hammurabi: King of Babylon

In 1792 B.C., Hammurabi, a descendant of Sumu-abum, became king of Babylon. He had visions of establishing Babylon as the capital of a new empire in Mesopotamia. To reach his goal, Hammurabi acted to bring about an end to the dangerous rivalry between the major city-states. But before he

This artist's illustration of Babylon shows what the city might have looked like during the reign of Nebuchadnezzar.

could attempt this, he first had to solidify his rule. One of his first acts as king was to issue an order that forgave people's debts. This, of course, made him popular with his subjects. Hammurabi added to his popularity by beautifying Babylon's temples, strengthening the city's fortifications, and improving the irrigation system.

Hammurabi proved to be a wise states-
man. For the first thirty-one years of his
reign, he made alliances with his rivals, broke
them when necessary, and renewed them
when it worked to his advantage. Finally,
Hammurabi went about unifying Mesopotamia. He waged war against the rival city-
states, one by one. First, he attacked and
defeated the city of Larsa, which allowed
him to gain control of southern and central
Mesopotamia. Next, he destroyed the city of
Mari, seizing control of western Mesopotamia. He then captured the cities of
Eshnunna, located about 65 miles north of
Babylon, and Assur, 200 miles northwest of
Babylon.

Having conquered his major rivals,
Hammurabi now ruled all of Mesopotamia
and some surrounding territory. His empire
extended all the way from the Persian Gulf in
the south to the southern part of present-day
Turkey, in the north, and from the Zagros

Mountains in the east to the Khabur River in present-day Syria. Hammurabi had proved to be a courageous military leader. Now he would demonstrate superb administrative skills in governing his vast empire.

The Code of Hammurabi

As a Mesopotamian king, Hammurabi was responsible for acting as a lawgiver and chief judge. Past kings of Mesopotamia had collections of laws, but

....

Hammurabi receiving his code of laws from the Sun-God. Hammurabi is at the left, standing before the god. The king had this sculpture carved at the top of a stone stele on which was inscribed his body of laws, c.1750 B.C.

This is one representation of King Hammurabi the Lawgiver.

HAMMURABI

few besides Hammurabi's have been found. Known as the "Code of Hammurabi," these 282 specific laws, written on a black stone eight feet high, reinforce the principle that government has a responsibility for what occurs in society, since the laws concern themselves with the well-being of the empire: with family relations, property issues, business conduct, and crime.

Hammurabi's laws were intended to apply uniformly to all citizens. In the prologue, inscribed on the same stone with the 282 laws, Hammurabi wrote that the gods had instructed him "to make justice appear in the land, to destroy the evil and the wicked that the strong might not oppress the weak, to rise like the sun-god . . . to give light to the land."[1]

However, there are instances where the laws reflected a code of justice that is harsh by today's standards, literally demanding "an

A modern day view of the Euphrates River in Turkey. Babylon was located on the banks of the Euphrates River.

eye for an eye, a tooth for a tooth." For
example:

> If a man has accused another man and has
> brought a charge of murder against him,
> but has not proved it, his accuser shall be
> put to death.

> If a son has struck his father, they shall cut
> off his hand.

> If an awilum [possibly a landowner or head
> of household] has put out the eye of a
> mar-awilim [son of an awilum], they shall
> put out his eye.[2]

The Code of Hammurabi was not
Mesopotamia's first collection of laws. One
of the oldest is the code of laws of the
Sumerian king Ur-Nammu, which dates
from about 2100 B.C. Only five of the laws,
of Ur-Nammu which were written on clay
tablets, have survived. Hammurabi's 282
laws were inscribed in forty-nine columns
on a basalt stela, or stone monument, and
became a permanent reminder for future

between
2 and 3

Bronze Foundation figure of Ur-Nammu. It depicts the king as a temple builder with a basket of earth to make bricks. It was made to be buried in the foundations of a temple. The copper "pegs" acting as a record for posterity and to receive the god's blessing.

civilizations that a complex society must be governed by law.

After Hammurabi's death in 1750 B.C., the Babylonian Empire began to crumble, following the usual Mesopotamian pattern. Hammurabi's descendants were unable to hold the empire together, as conflicts erupted again between rival city-states. The empire continued to shrink until it was reduced in size to the city of Babylon and the surrounding lands. Eventually, a new empire would arise in northern Mesopotamia.

Chapter 5

The ASSYRIAN EMPIRE

In about 1600 B.C., a people known as the Hittites, from Anatolia in what is now Turkey, invaded Mesopotamia. They swept down from the north and attacked and robbed the people of Babylon before returning to their homeland. The Hittite raid dealt a mortal blow to what remained of the former Babylonian Empire. Babylon and the rest of Mesopotamia were now so weak that the area was ripe for conquest.

The Kassite Conquest

Shortly after, the Kassites, another group who may have come from the Zagros Mountains or perhaps from as far away as central Asia, invaded Mesopotamia. A Kassite king, Agum-Kakrime, seized the throne of Babylon. The Kassites easily defeated the various Mesopotamian city-states and reunited them under Kassite rule. Their rule was not harsh: The Kassite rulers allowed the citizens of the former

Babylonian Empire to continue living just as they had been for hundreds of years. The Kassites also adopted the Babylonian culture and way of life, including the Babylonians' language. They rebuilt the temples and respected the Mesopotamian gods. The god of the city of Babylon, Marduk, became the god of all of Mesopotamia under Kassite rule.

The Kassites were also careful not to trample on citizens' rights that had long been established. For that reason, there were no rebellions against Kassite rule, which lasted for more than four hundred years. During their rule, the Kassites expanded trade with places as far away as Egypt, India, and Afghanistan. Meanwhile, the Assyrians in northern Mesopotamia, who had grudgingly accepted Kassite rule, found other ways to assert their influence. In 1365 B.C., Ashuruballit I became king of Assyria. He conquered part of a land to the

Assyrian archers in battle.

west of Assyria known as Mitanni. This conquest marked the beginning of Assyria's rise to power.

About 1170 B.C., the Elamites in what is now the country of Iran once again attacked Mesopotamia. They overthrew the last of the Kassite kings and stole whatever they could from Mesopotamia's cities. The loot that the Elamites carried home with them included the stone stela inscribed with the Code of Hammurabi as well as a statue of the god Marduk.[1]

The Rise of the Assyrians

The Assyrians excelled at war, perhaps more than any other Mesopotamian civilization. In 1115 B.C., the Assyrian king Tiglath-Pileser I set forth on a series of military campaigns. His many successes on the battlefield against enemies from all the surrounding lands restored Assyrian pride. But to his enemies, he inspired fear because

The Assyrians were the most skilled warriors of Mesopotamia. Pictured are Assyrian soldiers with shields and bows.

of his ruthlessness and brutality. In an inscription describing his victory over the Anatolians, Tiglath-Pileser wrote, "With their twenty thousand warriors and their five kings I fought . . . Their blood I let flow in the valleys and on the high levels of the mountains. I cut off their heads and outside their cities, like heaps of grain, I piled them up . . . I burned their cities with fire, I demolished them, I cleared them away . . ."[2]

The Assyrians gained a great deal of wealth through their military conquests, and since they now controlled trade routes, that wealth flowed back to the Assyrian capital of Assur. This gave Tiglath-Pileser the money he needed to rebuild the temples, restore the palaces, and improve Assyrian cities in other ways. But Assyria's rise to power was not always so easy. There were periods of decline, including about two hundred years following the reign of Tiglath-Pileser. During that period, invaders from neighboring lands seized parts of Assyria's territory. But the later Assyrian kings, including Assurnasirpal II, his son Shalmaneser III, and Tiglath-Pileser III, restored Assyria's lands and added new trade routes.

Conquering With Ferocity

Between 850 B.C. and 650 B.C., Assyrians conquered much of the Fertile Crescent including Babylonia, Syria, Israel, and Egypt. The Assyrian kings organized the conquered territories into an empire. They were able to hold on to their empire by using their vast armies to control the conquered peoples.

Assyrian warriors were ferocious in combat. Assyrian troops dressed in armor were given state-of-the-art weapons: iron-tipped spears, iron daggers and swords, and large iron shields. Assyrian battle tactics included using ladders to scale the walls of

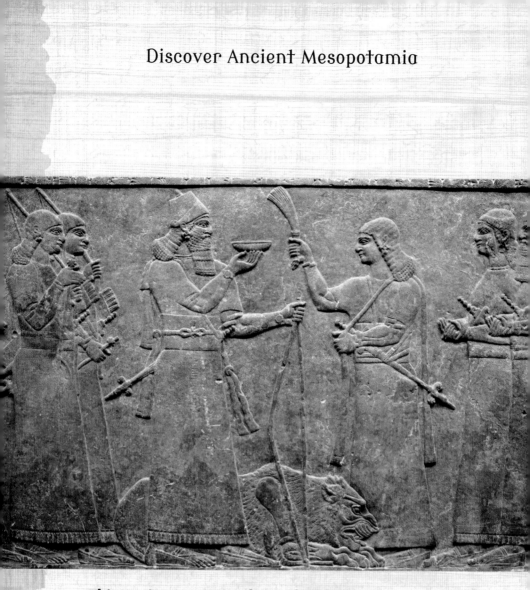

This ancient Assyrian bas-relief (865-860 B.C.) shows King Ashurbanipal accompanied by his courtiers pouring a libation over a dead lion.

an enemy's fortified cities and digging
tunnels to weaken the foundation of an
enemy's walls. Assyrian archers launched
waves of arrows against enemy soldiers
defending the city walls, and then other
fighters used heavy wooden beams covered
with iron tips to break through the city's
gates. The Assyrians warriors showed no
mercy to their defeated enemies. Those
who were not killed were enslaved.

Warrior-Kings of Assyria

In 689 B.C., the Assyrian king Sennacherib
destroyed the city of Babylon and many
other Mesopotamian cities and towns that
had dared to rebel against his rule. As the
crown prince, Sennacherib had gained
extensive experience fighting on the
northern frontier of the empire. He spent
most of his reign fighting to maintain the
empire established by his father, Sargon II.
Sennacherib would not be satisfied until

The remains of Nergal gate in Nineveh, Iraq, as seen on November 22, 2008. Nineveh, built between 704-681 B.C., was a capital of the Assyrian Empire and was surrounded by a 12-kilometer mud

Babylon was totally wiped out, as he expressed in these words.

> With [the inhabitants corpses] I filled the city squares ... The city and houses, from its foundation to its top, I destroyed, I devastated, I burned with fire. The wall and outer wall, temples and gods, temple-towers of brick and earth, as many as there were, I razed. ... Through the midst of that city I dug canals [from the Euphrates river], I flooded its site with water. ... That in days to come the site of that city, and [its] temples and gods, might not be recognized, I dissolved it in water, ... annihilated it, making it like a meadow.[3]

But like other warrior-kings before him, Sennacherib was a builder as well as a destroyer. He rebuilt the Assyrian capital at Nineveh on the Tigris River, near present-day Mosul, Iraq. He spared no expense in creating the largest, most impressive palace of its time. Assyrian artists in Nineveh created finely carved sculptures and panels depicting the lion hunt, a royal sport of

These portal guardians mark the entrance to the ruins of the northwest palace in the ancient city of Calah, now known as Nimrud in Iraq. Nimrud is a candidate to become a protected United Nations Educational, Scientific and Cultural Organization World Heritage site.

Assyrian kings, and Assyrian military victories in all their gruesome detail. Doorways were guarded by statues of huge winged bulls and sphinxes, mythological creatures with the head of a lion and the body of a man, ram, or hawk.

During the reign of King Ashurbanipal, from 668 to 627 B.C., the Assyrian Empire reached its high point. The lands under Assyrian control stretched all the way from Egypt to the Caucasus Mountains in what is today Armenia, a distance of more than one thousand miles. Ashurbanipal, who was a scholar as well as a military leader, was interested in preserving Mesopotamian culture. He collected twenty-five thousand clay cuneiform tablets from all over Mesopotamia for the magnificent library he built at Nineveh.

While the Assyrians basked in the glory of their massive wealth and power, trouble was erupting in Mesopotamia. The

An illustration of an Assyrian winged bull stands guard over a map highlighting the territory of ancient Assyria.

Assyrians had made many enemies in building their empire. Now, during the later years of Ashurbanipal's reign, revolts began breaking out in various parts of the realm. After the death of Ashurbanipal, the Assyrians were left without a strong leader. In 625 B.C., the

Chaldeans from the marshlands in the far south region of Mesopotamia, led by the Chaldean king Nabopolassar, captured Babylon. Then in 612 B.C., a combined army of Chaldeans, Medes from what is now Iran, and other groups attacked and destroyed many Assyrian cities and towns, including Nineveh. The Assyrian rise to power had been long and slow, but like other empires before it, the fall of Assyria was swift.

Chapter 6

The **CHALDEAN EMPIRE: BABYLON REBORN**

After the Chaldeans and their allies defeated the Assyrians, Babylon enjoyed a brief renaissance, or rebirth, that would last about sixty years. Under the Chaldeans, Babylon once again ruled an empire consisting of much of the territory that had been controlled by the Assyrians.

The Rule of Nebuchadnezzar II

The Chaldean king Nebuchadnezzar II, son of King Nabopolassar, like many rulers who preceded him, earned a reputation as both a builder and a destroyer. In 600 B.C., Nebuchadnezzar II made Babylon his capital. He rebuilt and enlarged the city, creating impressive new features, while renovating and beautifying existing structures. Nebuchadnezzar is credited with creating the Hanging Gardens of Babylon, long considered one of the seven wonders of the ancient world, although some archaeologists now believe those

5 **This illustration shows what the Hanging Gardens of Babylon may have looked like. It has long been considered one of the seven wonders of the ancient world.**

gardens were not actually in the ancient city. The seven-story three-hundred-foot-high ziggurat in Babylon may have inspired the biblical story of the Tower of Babel. From such towers, the priests of Chaldea

These beautiful glazed tiles symbolize a lion in three-dimensional shape from the gates of ancient Babylon. The lion is the symbol of Babylon and represents Ishtar, the goddess of fertility, love, and war.

observed the stars and kept detailed records of how the stars and planets would seem to change positions. Their observations formed the basis for both astronomy and astrology.

Nebuchadnezzar II soon became just as fearsome a tyrant as the warrior-kings of the earlier Assyrian Empire. In 597 B.C., there was a rebellion in the Jewish kingdom of Judaea, one of the many territories claimed by the Chaldeans. The Jews had stopped paying taxes to Babylon. Nebuchadnezzar's army captured Jerusalem and took ten thousand Jewish captives back to Babylon in chains. In 586 B.C., there was another rebellion in Jerusalem. Nebuchadnezzar responded by destroying the city. He burned the Temple of Solomon to the ground, and he also exiled all of the Jews remaining in Jerusalem to Babylon. Many scholars now think that the Old Testament of the Bible was first assembled during this period.

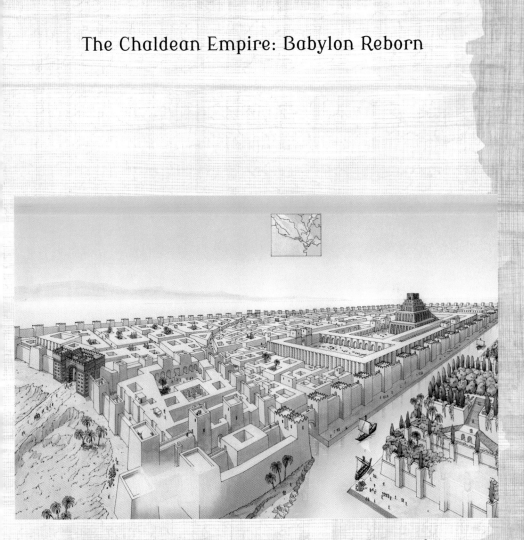

An artist's interpretation of what Babylon might have looked like. Note the Ishtar Gate in the foreground and ziggurat on the far right.

A single green ribbon spans the opening of a full size replica of the historic Ishtar Gate, the entryway to Babylon, before a ceremony to officially open it on February 27, 2011.

The Chaldean Empire: Babylon Reborn

In 562 B.C King Nebuchadnezzar II died. Following a familiar pattern, the Chaldean rulers who came next were too weak to hold the empire together. King Nabonidus, the last of the Chaldean rulers, made the mistake of trying to replace the Babylonian god Marduk with another god.[1] This created resentment among the people and further weakened the empire.

Developments in Mesopotamia were being carefully observed by the Persian king Cyrus the Great, who was in the process of building a huge empire to the east. In 539 B.C., Cyrus conquered Mesopotamia, and Babylon became part of the Persian Empire, which would become the world's largest empire of the time. During the next two thousand years, Mesopotamia would be ruled by a succession of different peoples including the Persians, Greeks, Romans, Arabs, and Turks. Mesopotamia's decline finally came in A.D. 1258, when

Mongol invaders from the east destroyed its extensive irrigation system. Although Mesopotamia would eventually cease to exist, the inventions of its people and the advances of its early civilizations live on.

TIMELINE

c. 10,000–7000 B.C.—Nomadic hunter-gatherers in northern Mesopotamia.

c. 7000 B.C.—First agricultural settlements in northern Mesopotamia.

c. 6500 B.C.–3700 B.C.—Ubaid culture in southern Mesopotamia.

c. 3000 B.C.—Sumerians in southern Mesopotamia begin development of world's first civilization. Advent of writing (Sumerian cuneiform script).

c. 2500 B.C.—Sumerians produce copper spearheads and body armor.

2800 B.C.–2350 B.C.—Constant warfare between Sumerian city-states.

2334 B.C.—Akkadian conquest of Sumer is completed by Sargon I, who then builds Akkadian Empire, world's first empire.

2200 B.C.—Akkadian Empire ends with attack by Gutians.

2140 B.C.—Sumerians take back control of Mesopotamian cities.

2000 B.C.—Elamites destroy city of Ur, bringing Sumerian rebirth to an end.

Discover Ancient Mesopotamia

c. 1792 B.C.–1750 B.C.—Hammurabi's rule: He
becomes king of Babylon, build Babylonian
Empire, and creates Code of Hammurabi
(282 laws).

1600 B.C.–1170 B.C. —Kassites rule Mesopotamia

1115 B.C.—Assyrian king Tiglath-Pileser begins
series of conquests, building Assyrian Empire.

689 B.C.—Assyrian king Sennacherib destroys
Babylon

668 B.C.–627 B.C.—Height of Assyrian Empire
under King Ashurbanipal.

612 B.C.—Chaldeans and Medes destroy Assyrian
cities, including Nineveh; end of Assyrian
Empire.

600 B.C.—Chaldean king Nebuchadnezzar 11 makes
Babylon his capital.

586 B.C.—Nebuchadnezzar II destroys Jerusalem,
burns Temple of Solomon, exiles Jews to
Babylon.

539 B.C.—Chaldean Empire ends when Persian king
Cyrus the Great conquers Mesopotamia.

GLOSSARY

A.D.—An abbreviation for the Latin anno Domini, meaning "in the year of our Lord." Used for a measurement of time, A.D. indicates the number of years since the supposed birth date of Christ.

archaeologist—A scientist who studies the remain of early people.

B.C.—Before Christ. Used for a measurement of time, B.C. indicates the number of years before the supposed birth date of Christ.

city-state—A city that is like an independent country. The cities of ancient Sumer were all city-states.

civilization—A kind of culture marked by a high level of organization in government and religion. Trade, writing, and are all part of civilization.

culture—A people's way of life.

cuneiform—A kind of writing done by making wedge-shaped marks on clay tablets.

domesticate—To change from a wild to a tame state.

dynasty—A series of rulers who belong to the same family.

empire—A nation and the countries it rules.

Discover Ancient Mesopotamia

Fertile Crescent—An area of fertile land in the shape of a half moon that lies between the Tigris and Euphrates rivers in Southwest Asia.

goddess—A female god; a being who was believed to have powers greater than a human being.

hunter-gatherer—A person who lives by gathering plants and hunting wild animals. Most early people used both of these ways to get food.

invade—To force one's way into.

irrigation—A method of bringing water to a field.

legend—A story of deeds of long ago which, while usually not true, has been believed by many people.

levee—A bank built to keep a river from overflowing.

myth—A story about gods and goddesses.

pictograph—a picture used as a sign or symbol.

scribe—A person who wrote down things for other people.

slave—a person who is owned by another.

stela—A carved or inscribed stone pillar.

ziggurat—A temple with huge square towers.

CHAPTER NOTES

Chapter 1. MESOPOTAMIA: LAND BETWEEN THE RIVERS

1. Stephen Bertman, *Handbook to Life in Ancient Mesopotamia* (New York: Facts on File, Inc., 2003), p. 203.
2. Samuel Noah Kramer, *Cradle of Civilization* (New York: Time-Life Books, 1967), p. 15.
3. Ibid., p. 31.

Chapter 2. SUMER: THE WORLD'S FIRST CIVILIZATION

1. Karen Rhea Nemet-Nejat, *Daily Life in Ancient Mesopotamia* (Westport, Conn.: Greenwood Press, 1998), p. 54.
2. Ibid., p. 66.
3. Stephen Bertman, *Handbook to Life in Ancient Mesopotamia* (New York: Facts on File, Inc., 2003), p. 194.
4. Nemet-Nejat, p. 102.
5. Bertman, p. 203.

Chapter 3. AKKAD: THE WORLD'S FIRST EMPIRE

1. Karen Rhea Nemet-Nejat, *Daily Life in Ancient Mesopotamia* (Westport, Conn.: Greenwood Press, 1998), p. 14.

2. Stephen Bertman, *Handbook to Life in Ancient Mesopotamia* (New York: Facts on File, Inc., 2003), pp. 264–265.
3. Editors of Time-Life Books, *Sumer: Cities of Eden* (Alexandria, Va.: Time-Life Books, 1993), p. 159.

Chapter 4. THE BABYLONIAN EMPIRE

1. Samuel Noah Kramer, *Cradle of Civilization* (New York: Time-Life Books, 1967), p. 53.
2. Joan Oates, *Babylon* (London: Thames and Hudson, 1979), pp. 74–75.

Chapter 5. THE ASSYRIAN EMPIRE

1. Samuel Noah Kramer, *Cradle of Civilization* (New York: Time-Life Books, 1967), p. 56.
2. Ibid., p. 57.
3. Ibid., p. 61.

Chapter 6. THE CHALDEAN EMPIRE: BABYLON REBORN

1. Samuel Noah Kramer, *Cradle of Civilization* (New York: Time-Life Books, 1967), p. 62.

FURTHER READING

BOOKS

Hunter, Erica. *Ancient Mesopotamia*. New York: Chelsea House, 2007.

McCaughrean, Geraldine *Gilgamesh the Hero*. Grand Rapids, MI: Eerdmans Books for Young Readers, 2003.

Moss, Carol. *Science in Ancient Mesopotamia*. London, U.K.: Franklin Watts, 1998.

Mountjoy, Shane. *The Tigris and Euphrates Rivers*. Philadelphia: Chelsea House, 2005.

Podany, Amanda H., and Marni McGee. *The Ancient Near Eastern World*. New York: Oxford University Press, 2005

Scholl, Elizabeth. *How'd They Do That? in Ancient Mesopotamia*. Hockessin, DE: Mitchell Lane Publishers, 2009.

Schomp, Viriginia. *Ancient Mesopotamia: The Sumerians, Babylonians, and Assyrians*. New York: Marshall Cavendish Benchmark, 2004.

Steele, Philip. *Eyewitness Mesopotamia*. New York : DK Publishing, Inc., 2007.

INTERNET ADDRESSES

Ancient Mesopotamia—Kids Konnect
<www.kidskonnect.com/.../history/257-ancient-mesopotamia.html>

Mesopotamia—The British Museum
<www.mesopotamia.co.uk>agriculture, 14-21, 34

INDEX